TARGETING THE REICH

A Mosquito in flight, 1943

TARGETING THE REICH

Allied Photographic Reconnaissance
over Europe, 1939–1945

ALFRED PRICE

Targeting the Reich
First published 2003 by Greenhill Books,
Lionel Leventhal Limited, Park House, 1 Russell Gardens, London NW11 9NN
www.greenhillbooks.com
and
Stackpole Books, 5067 Ritter Road, Mechanicsburg, PA 17055, USA

British Library Cataloguing in Publication Data
Price, Alfred
Targeting the Reich: Allied photographic reconnaissance over Europe, 1939-1945
World War, 1939-1945 - Europe - Reconnaissance
Aerial reconnaissance, American - Europe
Aerial reconnaissance, British - Europe
I. Title
940.5'44
ISBN 1-85367-546-6

Library of Congress Cataloging-in-Publication Data available

Designed by DAG Publications Ltd
Design by David Gibbons
Layout by Anthony A. Evans
Edited by Andy Oppenheimer
Printed in China

CONTENTS

PHOTOGRAPHIC RECONNAISSANCE

I depend on you, Spitfire, here in this world
   Of clear attenuated atmosphere.
The fields of France eight miles below
   The sky blue-black, mysterious, above
And trailing us, the traitorous path of mist
   For every Hun to see.

I depend on you, Spitfire. We have no guns
   To spit our hate at Me 109s.
Only our wits with which to dodge the Hun
   As, self-dependent like a hunted fox,
We set ourselves above the mark
   and watch our camera click.

Along together in the vastness of the sky
   The target for a hundred thousand eyes
In each of them the lust to kill
   That tiny, potent, speck that's you and me.
I realise now how the fox assuredly
   Disdains the efforts of the hounds.

Wing Commander Nigel Tangye

PREFACE

A long-respected military adage assures us: 'Time spent on reconnaissance is seldom, if ever, wasted.' To deploy a fighting force with greatest effect, a commander needs to have accurate intelligence on enemy dispositions, strengths and movements. Aerial reconnaissance (and today that includes satellite reconnaissance) is just one of many sources of intelligence, albeit an important one; others included reports from spies, the interrogation of prisoners, reports from own troops in front line positions, radar intercepts and decrypted and plain language radio transmissions from the enemy. Intelligence officers have the task of assembling the often disparate and sometimes conflicting items, and melding them into a coherent and usable picture. Put simply, their job is to convert information about the enemy into knowledge of the enemy.

During World War II the Royal Air Force published a journal entitled 'Evidence in Camera', containing a spread of interesting and dramatic photographs taken by reconnaissance aircraft or from combat cameras. Modern computerised printing technology has made it possible to lift selected photographs from that journal and reproduce them in this book without loss of quality. Taken together, these photographs convey a series of interesting peeks into the workings of the Third Reich, and of the Allies' increasingly effective efforts to dismantle it.

Fighters and bombers usually flew in formations as they went about their respective tasks. For their crews there was the excitement and spectacle of combat, the sight of falling enemy planes or targets destroyed. Compared with that, a lone reconnaissance aircraft sneaking past a target perhaps several weeks before an attack, and again after it, might have seemed an unnecessary appendage. Yet assuredly that was not the case. It was no exaggeration to say that without successful pre-strike reconnaissance, an air strike on a target of any complexity was unlikely to be effective. Without such reconnaissance, those planning an attack could only guess at the location of those parts of the target that were vulnerable. They could only conjecture on the strength and the layout of the defences around the target that might disrupt an attack. Similarly, without the later post-strike reconnaissance, the planners could not know with certainty whether their attack had been successful or if it needed repeating.

It required a special kind of courage to venture alone deep into enemy territory, to brave the defences and risk all to secure the precious pictures. The reader may gain a flavour of how it felt to fly this mission from Wing Commander Nigel Tangye's poem 'Photographic Reconnaissance', which precedes this Preface.

This book shows how the photographic reconnaissance process evolved in the Royal Air Force and, later, the US Army Air Forces, in Europe during World War II. It also conveys an idea of the wealth of the intelligence that was collected.

Alfred Price, Uppingham, Rutland

THE DEVELOPMENT OF PHOTOGRAPHIC RECONNAISSANCE, 1939 TO 1945

Left, upper picture: The Bristol Blenheim IV, with a maximum speed of 266 mph at 11,800 feet and a ceiling of about 24,000 feet, flew the first long-range photographic reconnaissance missions undertaken by the Royal Air Force during World War II. Heavy losses early in the war forced the service to abandon using the type for this role.

Left, lower picture: Five squadrons of Lysander tactical reconnaissance planes went to France with the British Expeditionary Force in 1939. The type had an excellent short field performance, but its maximum speed of only 230 mph meant it was extremely vulnerable to fighter attack.

At the outbreak of World War II, in September 1939, the RAF planned to use its twin-engined Bristol Blenheims to fly the long-range photographic reconnaissance mission. Short-range photographic missions in support of the army were to be flown by single-engined Westland Lysanders. Accordingly, when war broke out, four squadrons of Blenheims and five of Lysanders went to France as part of the Air Component of the British Expeditionary Force. Other Blenheims, belonging to Bomber Command and based in England, were to take the photographs necessary for targeting bombing attacks and for bomb damage assessment.

The RAF soon realised that with its current equipment, photographic reconnaissance was a far more costly business than it had anticipated. Between the start of the war and the end of 1939, Blenheims set out on 89 reconnaissance sorties into German airspace. Sixteen of those aircraft failed to return. Moreover, due to the frequent harassment from anti-aircraft guns and fighters, only about half the sorties yielded useful photographs.

The obvious lesson was that an unescorted Blenheim flying over enemy territory at heights between 10,000 and 20,000 feet, by day and in the clear skies needed for photography, had a poor chance of survival. Although they produced some useful photographs of portions of the German defences in the west, the cost had been great and the intelligence picture was far from complete. There were no photographs of the all-important Ruhr industrial area, or of targets deeper in German territory. The slow Lysander army-cooperation aircraft, intended to fly tactical reconnaissance missions to support the army, failed to produce any useful photographs of enemy territory.

If the RAF was not to fight its battles 'blind', it needed much better equipment to secure photographs of targets in enemy territory. Fortunately, in the autumn of 1939, a better system had already been proposed. Shortly before the outbreak of war, Flying Officer Maurice 'Shorty' Long-bottom had written a detailed memorandum on strategic aerial reconnaissance, which passed up the chain of command to the Air Ministry in London. In it he stated:

'This type of reconnaissance must be done in such a manner as to avoid the enemy fighters and AA defences as completely as possible. The best method of doing this appears to be the use of a single small machine, relying solely on its speed ... and ceiling to avoid detection.'

Today this concept is firmly accepted, but in 1939 it was a radical departure from the accepted thinking. Longbottom wanted to convert a high performance fighter plane – he suggested the Spitfire – into an unarmed high-speed high-flying reconnaissance aircraft. The latter would dart into enemy territory, take the photographs and speed home, all with a minimum of fuss and avoiding the defences whenever possible.

Longbottom went into detail on the modifications necessary to prepare the Spitfire for the long-range reconnaissance role. It would have to be stripped of its guns, radio and other unnecessary equipment, which would reduce its weight by about 450 pounds. Since a rapid rate of climb was unnecessary for a reconnaissance aircraft, he thought the proposed reconnaissance Spitfire could get airborne at an all-up-weight some 480 pounds heavier than the standard fighter version. That gave the modified Spitfire 930 pounds of lifting capacity for the battery of cameras and the extra fuel to extend its range. He argued that the reconnaissance version of the Spitfire could carry three times as much fuel as the standard fighter version, giving it a range of 1,500 miles.

Senior RAF officers read Longbottom's paper with interest, though initially nothing could be done to prove or disprove his arguments. The service was desperately short of modern fighters, particularly Spitfires, and the entire production of the latter was allocated to Fighter Command for the defence of Britain. At first Air Chief Marshal Sir Hugh Dowding, the head of Fighter Command, refused to release precious Spitfires for other roles no matter how persuasive the arguments.

The breakthrough for Longbottom's ideas came with the growing realisation that the RAF lacked any effective long-range photographic reconnaissance capability. Following strong representations from the Air Ministry, Dowding reluctantly agreed to release a couple of Spitfires for modification as reconnaissance aircraft. Two Mark I fighters off the production line were flown to Heston airfield north of London, for the highly secret reconnaissance unit known as the 'Heston Flight'. Wing Commander Sidney Cotton commanded the unit and, appropriately, one of the first officers posted in was 'Shorty' Longbottom himself.

The first priority was to carry out the minimum of modifications necessary to enable the Spitfire to photograph targets in enemy territory, and show there were no insurmountable problems if it was used in this role. In place of the wing-mounted guns and ammunition boxes, each Spitfire had two fixed F.24 cameras with 5-inch lenses mounted to look vertically downwards with a slight overlap in cover. The empty gun ports were covered with metal plates, then all joints in the airframe were filled with plaster of Paris and rubbed down to give a smooth finish and squeeze the

Right: Seclin, France, 18 November 1939. Flight Lieutenant Maurice 'Shorty' Longbottom about to take off on the first Spitfire photographic reconnaissance mission. The aircraft had had its armament removed, and an F.24 camera with 5-in lens installed in the gun bay in each wing.

last ounce of speed out of the aircraft. Due to the need to test the new concept as rapidly as possible, the first two reconnaissance Spitfires carried no additional fuel tanks.

Sydney Cotton devised a novel colour scheme for his Spitfires. Earlier, he had noticed that aircraft seen in the distance from below invariably appeared as a dark silhouette against the lighter background of the sky. Thus, he reasoned, at a distance a light coloured aircraft was less visible than a dark one. Cotton had his two Spitfires painted in a shade of pale green, which he thought would make them less conspicuous to an observer looking in their direction from below.

In the autumn of 1939 Cotton's unit was renamed 'No 2 Camouflage Unit' to explain the odd colouring of its Spitfires. One aircraft was detached to Seclin near Lille in France to begin operations. On 18 November 'Shorty' Longbottom, now a Flight Lieutenant, flew the first Spitfire reconnaissance mission. His target was the German city of Aachen and the fortifications nearby. As he ran through the target area at 33,000 feet he found that navigation was more difficult than expected, for while taking photographs with the wings horizontal he had no view of the ground below the aircraft. When his films were developed, they showed a strip of ground on the Belgian side of the frontier to the south of Aachen.

For his next mission Longbottom revised his technique, and planned to navigate through the target area using ground features more than ten miles away on either side of track. On the 22nd, he successfully photographed the Belgian-German border defences to the east of Liege.

During the six weeks that followed, long periods of cloud cover prevented high altitude photography of enemy territory. Then at the end of December the skies cleared sufficiently to allow the Spitfires to resume their operations. In short order they photographed Aachen, Cologne, Kaiserslautern, Wiesbaden, Mainz and parts of the Ruhr. Significantly, this was done without loss and with little interference from fighters or AA guns.

By the end of 1939, the two Spitfires had flown fifteen sorties without loss. Moreover, two-thirds of their sorties yielded photographs of enemy territory. Of the five abortive Spitfire sorties, four were due to cloud cover at the target and only one was due to enemy interference. The flights proved the soundness of Longbottom's concept for using the Spitfire for reconnaissance, and Air Chief Marshal Dowding reluctantly agreed to release a dozen more of these precious fighters for the new role.

Those early experimental flights pointed out the path for the future of long range photographic reconnaissance, but some major problems remained to be overcome. Foremost among these was the fact that the Spitfire's high altitude performance exceeded the capabilities of the cameras it carried. The F.24, the RAF's standard reconnaissance camera in 1939, had been designed more than a decade earlier to photograph targets from altitudes around 10,000 feet. From there, its 5-inch lens provided photographs with a scale of 1:24,000. This meant that 1 inch on the print represented 660 yards on the ground, sufficient to allow photo interpreters to identify military installations, troop positions and individual vehicles. When the F.24 took photographs from a Spitfire at 30,000 feet, it produced prints with a scale of 1:72,000. This meant that 1 inch on the print represented just over a mile on the ground, which was too small for the interpreters to extract much useful military intelligence from the pictures. Enlargement of the prints did not solve the problem because the details sought – typically troops positions, individual vehicles or bomb damage – were about the same size as the grain of the film and could not be seen even using high magnification.

Another problem was that of having cameras freeze up during

flight at high altitude. That difficulty was cured by ducting hot air from the engine cooling system through the camera bays.

In January 1940 a slightly improved photographic reconnaissance version of the Spitfires became available, the PR IB. To distinguish it from the earlier variant, the latter was renamed the PR IA. The PR IB carried one 8-inch focal lens camera in each wing, giving a useful improvement in the scale of the photographs (1:45,000 from 30,000 feet) compared with those taken with 5-inch lens cameras. Also, the PR IB carried an extra 29-gallon fuel tank in the rear fuselage to give a useful increase in range.

In February 1940 'Shorty' Longbottom demonstrated the improved capability of the PR IB when, taking off from Debden in Essex, he photographed the important German naval bases at Wilhelmshaven and Emden. In the following month, one of these aircraft photographed almost the whole of the Ruhr industrial area in a single flight. The mosaic made of prints taken during that sortie would become the standard briefing aid for sorties over this all-important area.

During the early Spitfire operations, Cotton's light green camouflage scheme was found to be too light for operations at high altitude. A medium blue scheme was therefore adopted and it became standard for all high-flying RAF reconnaissance planes.

Also during the early part of 1940, Cotton's unit was renamed the Photographic Development Unit (PDU). For the first time, its title to revealed the true nature of the unit's activities. Early in 1940 the reconnaissance operations in France were formalised and a new unit, No 212 Squadron, was created at Seclin to fly them.

The reconnaissance Spitfire underwent further modification. In March 1940 the PR 1C appeared, with a 30-gallon blister tank under the port wing, counterbalanced by a pair of cameras with 8-inch lenses in a similar blister under the starboard wing. With the extra a 29-gallon tank in the rear fuselage, this version carried 59 gallons more fuel than the fighter version.

On 7 April 1940, 'Shorty' Longbottom flew the prototype PR IC to Kiel. His photographs revealed numerous ships in the harbour, and lines of Junkers 52 transport planes drawn up on the nearby airfield at Holtenau. Since there had been no previous photography of the port or the airfield, it was impossible to know whether those concentrations were normal or if they signified that a large-scale operation was in the offing. Two days later German troops invaded Denmark and Norway, and the significance of concentrations become clear. The incident demonstrated the vital need for regular reconnaissance of important targets, so that major changes in dispositions would be recognisable.

Just over a month later, on 10 May 1940, German forces launched their powerful *Blitzkrieg* attack on France, Holland and Belgium. During the hectic weeks that followed, No 212 Squadron flew numerous sorties

Left: Flight Lieutenant Maurice 'Shorty' Longbottom (right) had proposed the use of the Spitfire for the long-range photographic reconnaissance role before the war, and flew the initial operational sorties with this type.

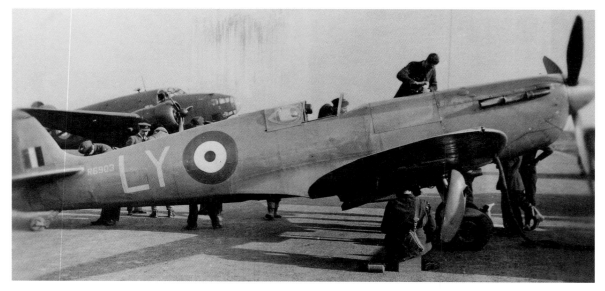

charting the relentless progress of the German Panzer columns through France. The latter quickly reached the English Channel, slicing the defending allied army into two.

The Spitfires' photographs could do nothing to avert defeat. However, by keeping Allied commanders aware of the enormity of their predicament, this source of intelligence prompted a timely start to preparations for the successful evacuation of troops from Dunkirk. It is no exaggeration to say that the photographs from the reconnaissance Spitfires played a major part in preventing the defeat in France from becoming an irretrievable disaster.

After No 212 Squadron withdrew to England, the unit disbanded and its surviving aircraft and personnel were incorporated into the PDU at Heston. In July 1940, the PDU underwent yet another name change, and became the Photographic Reconnaissance Unit (PRU). At the same time, Wing Commander Geoffrey Tuttle replaced Sidney Cotton as commander. The changes of name and commander made no difference to the way the unit operated, however.

At the end of July a further Spitfire reconnaissance variant appeared, the PR 1F. This carried a 30-gallon blister tank under each wing and a 29-gallon tank behind the pilot, giving 89 gallons more than the fighter version. To provide additional oil for the increased duration of its flights, the new variant carried an enlarged oil tank beneath the engine. The cameras, mounted in the rear fuselage, initially comprised two F.24s with 8-in lenses. Later these were replaced by cameras with 20-inch focal lenses, which gave a further improvement in the scale of photographs (1:18,000 from 30,000 feet). The additional fuel increased the radius of action of the PR IF by about 100 miles, compared with the PR IC. Exploit-

Above: Spitfire PR IC. This variant was fitted with an additional 30-gallon blister tank under the port wing, and a 29-gallon tank in the rear fuselage. Counterbalancing the fuel tank on the port side was a blister under the starboard wing, seen here open, which covered a pair of F.24 cameras with 8-in lenses. In April 1940 one of these aircraft carried out the first photographic reconnaissance mission of Kiel harbour in Germany.

ing the additional range to the full, a PR IF flew the first photographic reconnaissance sortie to Berlin.

In the summer and autumn of 1940, reconnaissance Spitfires kept close watch on the progress of German preparations for the invasion of Britain. In those perilous times the PRU, with a strength comparable to a normal RAF fighter squadron, made a contribution to the national defence far greater than any other unit of comparable size. Each day when the weather allowed, its Spitfires photographed every German-occupied port along the Channel Coast. The regular counts of ships and barges at each port provided vital intelligence on the progress of the German invasion preparations.

At this time the British operation to decrypt high-grade German signals traffic, code-named 'Ultra', was producing a stream of useful information on German plans and deployments. Unknown to their pilots, a growing number of Spitfire reconnaissance sorties were targeted as follow-ups to Ultra decrypts. Once the Germans had seen a British reconnaissance aircraft pass over a particular area, whether or not its cameras had seen anything useful, British knowledge of activity there was assumed. Thus on many occasions, the Spitfires' sorties helped preserve the secrecy of the cipher breakers successes.

During the great air battle on 15 September 1940, Battle of Britain Day, the losses inflicted on the Luftwaffe convinced Hitler that RAF Fighter Command would not be defeated before the weather broke in the autumn. Accordingly, the Führer gave orders that the invasion be postponed until the following year. On 20 September, a reconnaissance Spitfire returned from Cherbourg with the first photographic evidence of the German change of plan, showing that five destroyers and a torpedo boat had left the port. In the weeks that followed, successive photographic sorties

Right: Wing Commander Geoffrey Tuttle assumed command of the Photographic Reconnaissance Unit at Heston in June 1940. He is pictured receiving the OBE from the King during a parade at the airfield that August.

revealed progressive reductions in the numbers of ships and barges assembled at the invasion ports. The threat to the nation had passed.

TO THE BALTIC AND THE MEDITERRANEAN

The Types C and F reconnaissance versions of the Spitfire opened new vistas for reconnaissance, yet with more extensive changes the modified fighter could do even better. The Supermarine Company re-designed the entire leading edge of fighter's wing to form a large integral fuel tank with a capacity of 114 gallons. In October 1940 the new Spitfire variant appeared, designated the PR ID. With a 29-gallon tank in the rear fuselage, it had a total internal fuel capacity of 228 gallons – two and a half times more than the standard Mark I fighter. In the rear fuselage the PR 1D carried two 8-inch or two 20-inch focal length cameras.

The additional tankage of the PR ID gave a dramatic increase in the area of German-held territory where it could operate. On 29 October 1940 a PR ID photographed the port of Stettin on the Baltic (now Sczecin in Poland) and returned after 5 hours and 20 minutes airborne. Other remarkable missions followed in rapid succession: to Marseilles and Toulon in the south of France, and to Trondheim in Norway.

When carrying its full load of fuel the PR ID was not an easy aircraft to fly, however. Flight Lieutenant Neil Wheeler, one of the early Spitfire reconnaissance pilots, recalled:

'You could not fly it straight and level for the first half hour or hour after take-off. Until you had emptied the rear tank, the aircraft hunted the whole time. The centre of gravity was so far back that you couldn't control it. It was the sort of thing that would never have got in during peacetime, but war is another matter.'

Below: The Spitfire PR ID, later redesignated the PR Mark IV. This variant carried 133 gallons of extra fuel in a tank built integrally with the leading edge of the wing, which gave rise to the unusual spectacle of a Spitfire being refuelled almost at the wing tip.

As the rear fuel tank emptied, the Spitfire's normally pleasant handling characteristics gradually returned.

OBLIQUE CAMERAS

Initially the reconnaissance Spitfires photographed their targets from vertically above, from medium or high altitude. Most photography would continue to be done that way but another technique, using a fixed oblique-mounted camera, allowed close-up shots to be taken of small targets from low altitude. The technique also allowed aircraft to photograph targets from below a blanket of low cloud.

The first Spitfire fitted with the fixed oblique camera installation was the PR IE. This aircraft had a streamlined fairing under each wing, which housed an F.24 camera with a 5-inch lens pointing downwards at 13 degrees to the horizontal, and outwards at right angles to the line of flight. This installation was not successful, however, and only one Spitfire was so modified. It was soon replaced by the Type G, which became the main variant used for low altitude photography. The PR IG retained the fighter's armament of eight .303-inch machine guns, to give a self-defence capability if it encountered enemy fighters. The PR IG carried a three-camera installation in the rear fuselage comprising one 5-inch oblique camera looking to port, and one 14-inch and one 5-inch lens camera mounted vertically. To provide some extra range this variant carried a 29-gallon fuel tank in the rear fuselage. A few PR IGs were finished in normal day fighter camouflage, but the majority were painted a very pale shade of pink, barely off-white, which was effective in concealing them if they flew immediately below a layer of cloud. When there was no cloud cover, however, this colour scheme made the aircraft highly conspicuous from above.

Below: A pink painted Spitfire PR IG, later redesignated the PR Mark VII, used for low altitude photography below cloud. The window for the oblique F.24 camera is near the top of the outer ring of the fuselage roundel. This variant also carried two vertical cameras in the rear fuselage.

In November 1940 the Photographic Reconnaissance Unit was redesignated No 1 Photographic Reconnaissance Unit, to distinguish it from No 2 Photographic Reconnaissance Unit then forming in the Mediterranean theatre. Soon afterwards, No 1 PRU moved from Heston to Benson near Oxford, a permanent RAF airfield that would remain its base for the rest of the war.

Despite the progressive improvements made to the early reconnaissance Spitfires, life was never comfortable for their pilots. Pilot Officer Gordon Green, who flew with the PRU during 1941, commented:

'During the early [photographic reconnaissance] missions there was no such thing as cockpit heating in our Spitfires. For the high altitude missions we wore thick suits with electrical heating. Trussed up in our Mae West and parachute, one could scarcely move in the narrow cockpit of the Spitfire.

'When flying over enemy territory one had to be searching the sky the whole time for enemy fighters. On more than one occasion I started violent evasive action to shake off a suspected enemy fighter, only to discover that it was a small speck of dirt on the inside of my Perspex canopy!

'A big worry over enemy territory was that one might start leaving a condensation trail without knowing it, thus pointing out one's position to the enemy. To avoid that we had small mirrors fitted in the blisters on each side of the canopy, so that one could see the trail as soon as it started to form. When that happened one could either climb or descend until the trail ceased. If possible, we liked to climb above the trail's layer because then fighters trying to intercept us had first to climb through the trail's layer themselves and could be seen in good time.'

KEEPING WATCH ON THE GERMAN FLEET

Early in 1941, following a destructive foray into the north Atlantic to attack British shipping, the German battle cruisers *Scharnhorst* and *Gneisenau* and the heavy cruiser *Admiral Hipper* put into harbour at Brest in western France. If these warships put to sea again, the Admiralty needed to know as soon as possible so it could concentrate forces to meet the threat. No 1 PRU received a top priority task to photograph the port three times each day. To provide the best chance of achieving that requirement, whatever the weather, pairs of Spitfires took off from St Eval in Cornwall and flew to Brest independently. One of the aircraft was a blue-painted Type C or Type F, which ran in at high altitude to photograph the port if the skies were sufficiently clear. The other aircraft was a pale pink Type G, which ran in to photograph the port from low altitude if there was a blanket of cloud. For this assignment six-tenths' cloud was regarded as 'no-man's land': too much cloud to permit much chance of

Right: Map showing the rapid increases in the radius of action of successive versions of reconnaissance Spitfires, between March and October 1940. The map shows the combat radii for aircraft operating from Heston near London, Benson near Oxford, St Eval in Cornwall or Wick in Scotland. The Spitfire PR 1C appeared in March 1940 and could reach as far as Kiel in Germany. The PR 1F, the next major variant, entered service in July 1940 and could reach as far as Marseilles in the south of France. The PR 1D, the definitive Mark 1 reconnaissance variant, entered service in October 1940 and could reach as far as Stettin on the Baltic coast. The low-flying armed reconnaissance variant of the Spitfire, the PR 1G, carried less fuel than the C, D or F variants and its coverage extended only to the north coast of France and a small distance inland.

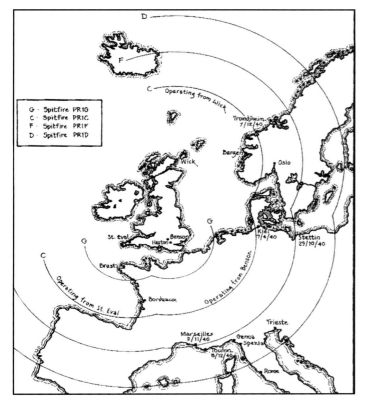

successful photography from high altitude, and too little to conceal a pink Spitfire running in below cloud. If there was insufficient cloud cover, the pilots flying the low-altitude PR 1Gs were ordered to abandon their mission.

The fighter units and flak batteries defending Brest soon realised that the RAF was mounting regular flights to photograph the harbour, and prepared accordingly. Gordon Green recounted:

'During the early [photographic reconnaissance] missions to cover Brest we lost about five pilots fairly quickly. After the first couple had failed to return the Flight Commander, Flight Lieutenant Keith Arnold, asked Benson to send some reserve pilots. They duly arrived. Both took off for Brest that evening and neither came back. That was a very sobering incident.

'The important thing with any photographic mission was to take the photos if one could, and get them back to base. As the "boss" of PRU, Wing Commander Geoffrey Tuttle, often used to say "I want you to get home safely not just because I like your faces, but because if you don't the whole sortie will be a waste of time!" So it was no use trying to play hide and seek with the Luftwaffe. If one had lost surprise during the approach to a heavily defended target, the best thing was to abandon the mission. One could go back another time when things might be better.

'Looking back at my time with the PRU, I get a lot of satisfaction from the knowledge that although I played my part in the war, I never had to fire a shot in anger. In one sense we in the reconnaissance business had things easy. All the time it was impressed on us: bring back the photographs or, if you can't, bring back the aeroplane. An infantryman taking part in the Battle of Alamein could not suddenly decide "This is ridiculous, I'm going home!" He just had to go on. But if we thought we had lost the element of surprise we were not only permitted to turn back, we were expected to do so.

'On the other hand, there were times when I knew real fear. When one was 15 minutes out from Brest on a low altitude sortie, one's heart was beating away and as the target got nearer one's mouth got completely dry.

Anyone who was not frightened at the thought of going in to photograph one of the most heavily defended targets in Europe, was not human.

'Whenever it was possible to photograph a target, flak could engage us: if we could see to photograph they could see to open up at us. But throughout my time as a reconnaissance pilot my luck held. I never once saw an enemy fighter, nor was my aircraft ever hit by flak. Indeed only once during the time we were flying those missions over Brest did one of our aircraft come back with any damage, and that was minor. It was all rather like a foxhunt – either the fox got away unscathed or else it was caught and killed. There was rarely anything in between.'

During 1941 there was a rationalisation of the system of designating the reconnaissance Spitfires then in service. The Type D became the PR Mark IV; the Type F became the PR Mark VI and the Type G became the PR Mark VII (by then the earlier reconnaissance Spitfires had been modified into Fs or Gs, or had passed out of service). Also during that year each reconnaissance Spitfire in front line service was fitted or retrofitted with the more powerful Merlin 45 series engine. No change in designation followed this change, however.

Towards the end of 1941 the twin-engined Mosquito entered service in the photographic reconnaissance role, thus opening vast new areas including Eastern Germany, the Baltic ports and much of Northern Norway. The carriage of a navigator in the Mosquito made it much easier to find distant targets, especially on flights involving a long sea crossing.

From the beginning of 1942 the German air defences steadily improved with the deployment of the latest Messerschmitt Bf 109G and FW 190A fighters. As a result, the reconnaissance units suffered mounting losses. The obvious answer was fit the new Rolls Royce Merlin 61 engine, with a two-stage supercharger, into reconnaissance versions of the Spitfire and

Above: In September 1941, the de Havilland Mosquito entered service in the photographic reconnaissance role. With greater range than the Spitfire, it opened to photography most of the rest of eastern Germany, the Baltic ports and northern Norway. The carriage of a navigator made it much easier to find the most distant targets, especially if the flight there involved a long sea crossing.

the Mosquito to improve their performance at high altitude. In the spring of 1943 the new variants entered service as the Spitfire XI and the Mosquito IX, able to photograph targets from 41,000 feet and 36,000 feet respectively. These aircraft enjoyed about a year of near-immunity from fighter interception provided they remained at high altitude. When these planes were lost it was usually after they had descended due to a technical failure, or the need to avoid condensation trails or to fly beneath cloud to take photographs.

Also during 1942 there were important developments in aerial cameras. This work culminated in the superb F.52 camera, fitted with lenses up to 36 inches long, which produced photographs to a scale of about 1:13,000 from 40,000 feet. That was sufficient to allow photo interpreters to observe and analyse, for example, the type of traffic in a railway siding, the state of construction of a U-boat or the layout of a radar installation.

As the war progressed, the RAF reconnaissance force faced increasing demands to provide photographs of targets deep inside occupied Europe. To meet these requirements, No 1 PRU steadily grew larger, so that by May 1942 it possessed six flights of Spitfires and two of Mosquitos with a total of 65 aircraft. That October No 1 PRU was re-organised into No 540 Squadron with Mosquitoes, and Nos 541, 542 and 543 Squadrons with Spitfires.

In August 1943 the US 8th Air Force established its own photographic reconnaissance unit, the 7th Photo Group, at Mount Farm near Benson. From the start there was very close co-operation between them and United States Army Air Force (USAAF) reconnaissance units, with much interchange of equipment and sharing of knowledge. Initially the 7th Photo Group flew F-5 aircraft, the reconnaissance version of the P-38 Lightning fighter. This aircraft was vulnerable to interception during deep penetrations into enemy territory, however, and it had serviceability problems. One squadron in the Group received Spitfire PR XIs, and operated these aircraft for the rest of the conflict.

Below: The Spitfire PR XI, powered by the Merlin 61 engine with two-stage supercharger, entered service at the end of 1942. This type proved highly successful, and it bore the brunt of the Allied photographic reconnaissance effort during the mid-war period. This example belonged to the US 7th Photo Group based at Mount Farm near Oxford.

Also in the latter part of 1943 the Mosquito PR XVI appeared, fitted with a pressurised cabin. It was an important innovation, which allowed its crews to remain alert and reasonably comfortable while flying for long periods at altitudes above 35,000 feet.

During the spring of 1944 the 654th Reconnaissance Squadron, part of the US 801st Reconnaissance Group based at Watton in Norfolk, formed with Mosquito XVIs. This unit flew photographic reconnaissance missions for the remainder of the war.

The period of near-invulnerability to interception for aircraft powered by the Merlin 61 engine lasted until the spring of 1944. It ended when with the appearance of the first German jet fighter types, the rocket-propelled Messerschmitt 163 and the turbojet powered Messerschmitt 262. The reconnaissance Spitfires and Mosquitos, flying alone and unarmed, offered perfect targets for the German jet pilots to carry out practice interceptions. Yet again losses began to rise.

THE MASTER SPY

To provide give a further increase in performance at high altitude, to reduce the threat of interception by the jet fighters, the Supermarine Company produced the definitive long-range unarmed reconnaissance variant of the Spitfire, the PR 19. (In 1943 the RAF had changed from roman to arabic mark numbers for all new aircraft types and new variants.) Driven by a 2,035 horsepower Rolls Royce Griffon engine, the new

Left: Ground crewman loading an F.52 camera with a 36-in lens into the cramped rear fuselage of a Spitfire PR 19. The film magazine, sitting on the trolley, was attached to the top of the camera after the latter was in place.

Right: The defini-
tive reconnais-
sance version of
the Spitfire, the
PR 19 powered by
the 2,035 horse-
power Rolls Royce
Griffon engine,
entered service in
the late spring of
1944. Fitted with a
pressurised cabin,
this formidable
aircraft was able to
photograph targets
from altitudes
above 48,000 feet.

Spitfire had integral wing tanks similar to those fitted to the PR IV and the PR XI. The first Mark 19s entered service in May 1944 and gave a huge advance in performance over their predecessors. After the first small batch, these aircraft were fitted with pressurised cabins which enabled pilots to operate for long periods at altitudes above 45,000 feet.

Provided the pilot of a Spitfire PR 19 saw an approaching enemy jet fighter in time, he had little difficulty in outmanoeuvring it. Squadron Leader Alfred Ball, commander of No 542 Squadron, recalled:

'I encountered Messerschmitt 262s on a couple of occasions. Unless your eyes were shut when they jumped you, you could usually get away from them. They had a long climb to reach us, and they could not stay with us for very long. I would wait until the 262 pilot was about to open fire, then pull into a tight turn. You had to judge the turn correctly – if you turned too soon it was not difficult for him to pull enough deflection and you were a sitting duck. Provided you handled your aircraft properly, it was very difficult for them to shoot you down.'

For low altitude reconnaissance a fighter-reconnaissance version of the Spitfire XIV fighter appeared. Also powered by a Griffon engine, it carried an oblique camera in the rear fuselage and was designated the FR XIV. This aircraft retained the fighter's armament of two 20-mm cannon and four machine guns, making a formidable opponent if engaged by enemy fighters.

Another high-performance reconnaissance type introduced near the end of the war was the F-6, the reconnaissance version of the famous P-51 Mustang fighter. In January 1945 a few of these aircraft were delivered to the US 7th Photo Group, which used the type for low altitude missions.

Throughout the war, there had also been many improvements in camera design. As aircraft speeds increased, blurring often appeared on close-up oblique photographs. To overcome this problem, some F.24 and F.52 cameras were modified into moving film strip cameras. In these, the film was arranged to pass over a narrow slit positioned near the focal plane, at a speed that cancelled out the movement of the aircraft. The resultant negative took the form of a continuous strip.

American reconnaissance cameras also made their appearance in USAAF and RAF planes, notably the K.17 with a 6-inch lens and the K.8 AB with a 12-inch lens, both for aerial survey and mapping. Another import innovation was the K.19 camera specially designed for night photography.

The night reconnaissance operation deserves mention at this stage. By 1944 the degree of the Allied air superiority over northwest Europe was such that whenever possible the German army made most of its troop movements at night. Two squadrons, Nos 69 and 140 equipped respectively with Wellington and Mosquito aircraft, provided the RAF 2nd Tactical Air Force with its night photographic capability.

The procedure for night photography, using a pair of K.19 cameras, was as follows. The aircraft approached the target at altitudes of around 10,000 feet, with the cameras' shutters locked in the 'open' position. As it neared the target, the plane released a line of M 46 photoflash bombs at about 10-second intervals. When the first flash bomb ignited at about 4,000 feet above the ground, it produced a brilliant flash of brief duration which lit up the ground and produced an image on the film. That flash triggered a photoelectric cell fitted to the cameras, which closed the shutters, wound on the film and then re-opened the shutters ready for the next picture. As each succeeding photo flash bomb ignited, the process was repeated.

AT THE WAR'S END

At the end of World War II in Europe the Royal Air Force and USAAF reconnaissance units were well-equipped and highly efficient collectors of intelligence. Their aircraft had the range to photograph targets anywhere in enemy held Europe, and the speed and the altitude performance to execute that task with minimal losses. Photographic reconnaissance had indeed made giant strides during the five years of conflict, and in the pages to follow the reader will see the fruits of those endeavours.

Above: Scale mattered. The village at Bullingen in Belgium (centre right of the picture, nearly halfway up), photographed by 'Shorty' Longbottom during his initial mission on 18 November 1939. Taken from 33,000 feet using an F.24 camera with a 5-in lens, the scale is about 1:79,000. Little ground detail is visible and individual vehicles or troop positions could not be picked out.

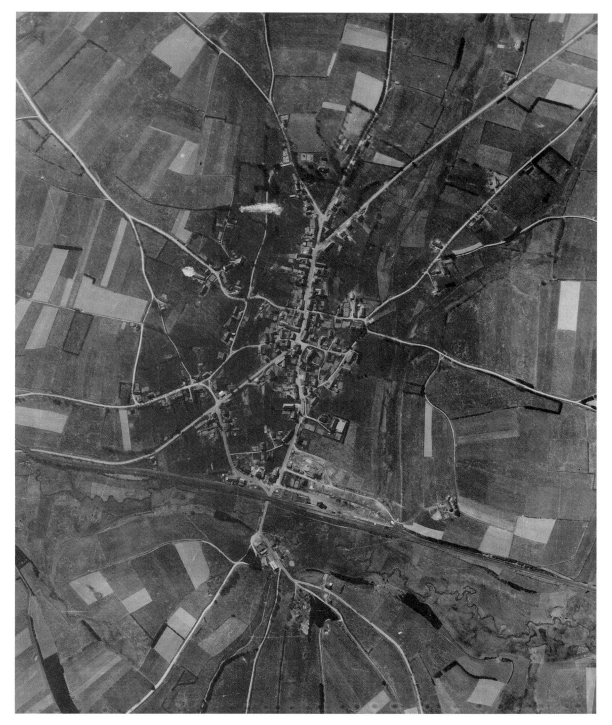

Contrast the 1939 photograph on page 24 with this one of the same village taken in April 1944, from a Spitfire at about the same altitude but using an F.52 camera with a 36-in lens. The scale is about 1:11,000. The later photo shows considerably more ground detail, and serves to indicate the advances made in the design of aerial cameras during the war years.

Picture of impending defeat. Taken from a reconnaissance Spitfire a few days after the end of the evacuation from Dunkirk early in June 1940, this photo shows more than a hundred German tanks and other vehicles moving towards Paris from the north. Soon afterwards Paris was declared an open city, and it surrendered to German forces on 14 June.

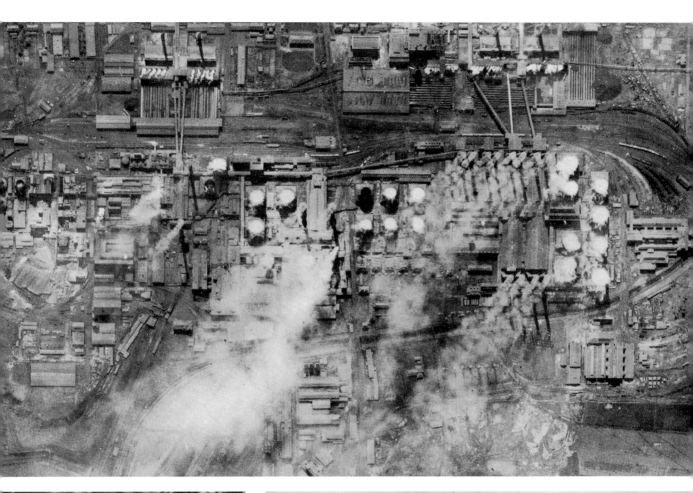

The Knapsack power station, 7 miles to the southwest of Cologne, was an important source of electricity for the Ruhr industrial area. On 12 August 1941, a force of 54 Blenheim bombers carried out a daring low-altitude attack on this and the nearby electrical generating plant at Quadrath. Ten bombers failed to return.

Below: Low-level oblique photographs of the Royal Dutch Blast Furnace and Steel Works at Ijmuiden, showing the plant's vulnerable features in detail.

Opposite page: In addition to those carried by specialised reconnaissance aircraft, Allied bombers also carried strike cameras to record the results of attacks. These photographs were taken during the daylight low-level attack on the Royal Dutch Steel Works at Ijmuiden, by four RAF Boston bombers of Nos 88 and 107 Squadrons on 27 November 1942. All the planes returned safely.

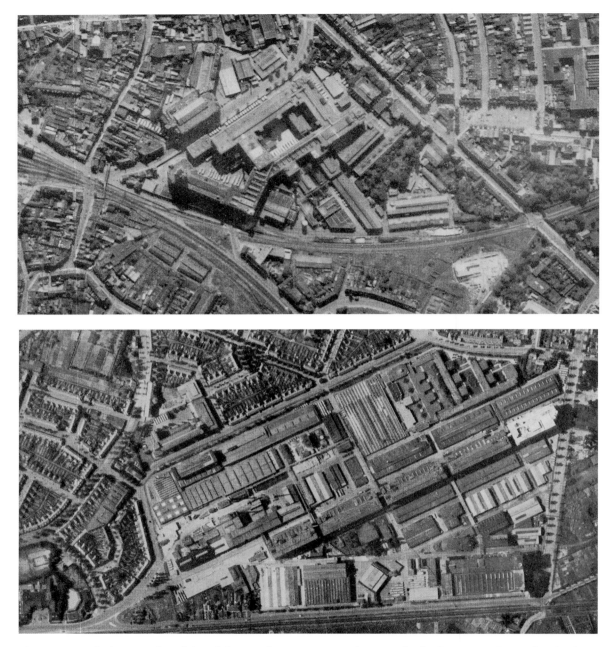

Above: Vertical photographs of the Philips Radio Works at Eindhoven in Holland, which in 1942 included the largest radio valve and lamp manufacturing plant in Europe. It produced a sizeable proportion of these items supplied to the German armed forces. The head office (above), included the lamp and valve manufacturing plant. The main part of the works (below) was situated about a quarter of a mile to the northwest of the head office and manufactured complete radio sets.

As can be seen, both plants were located in built-up parts of the city.

Opposite page: Operation 'Oyster', the attack on the Philips Works at Eindhoven on 6 December 1942, was mounted on a Sunday to minimise casualties among the Dutch work force. Ninety-two Venturas, Bostons and Mosquitoes took part in the daylight precision attack, and a Mosquito photographed the results. Fourteen bombers were lost in the attack.

Oppopsite page: The raid on the Philips Works caused severe damage to both parts of the factory.

Above: View of the Philips Works taken half an hour after the attack, showing the fires well ablaze. It was several months before the plant resumed full production.

Opposite page: The German naval ammunition depot at Mariensiel near Wilhelmshaven, photographed before 27 January 1943.

Above: On 27 January 1943 the US 8th Air Force attacked Germany for the first time, when 55 Boeing B-17 Flying Fortresses bombed the Mariensiel depot. As can be seen from this post-strike photograph, the bombs had set off large quantities of munitions and wrecked several storage bunkers at 'A'. Blast caused damage throughout the area outlined with a dashed line 'B', extending as far as the fuel storage tanks at 'C' on the opposite side of the basin.

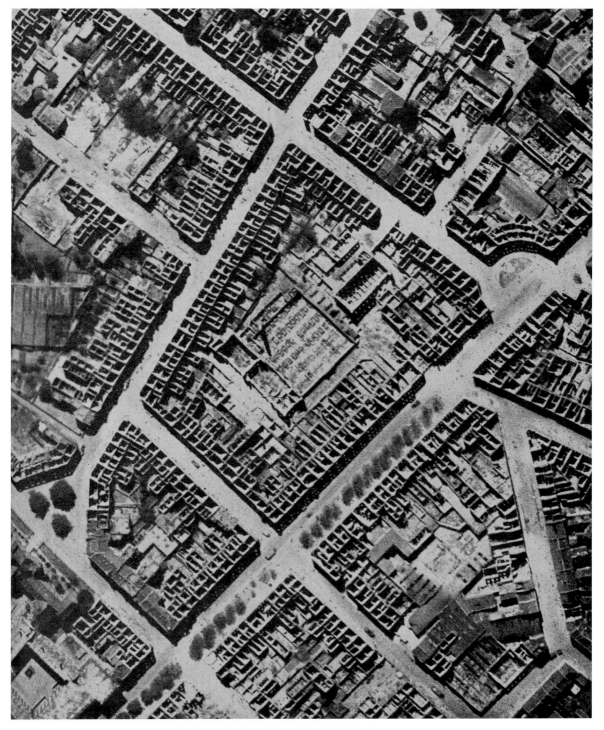

Opposite page: Pre-strike photo of part of the city of Aachen.

Above: Post-strike photo of the same area, following the attack by 374 aircraft of RAF Bomber Command on the night of 13/14 July 1943. Within the area depicted, scarcely a single house has its roof intact.

Below: The attack on the German dams, on 17 May 1943, was one of the epic air actions of the conflict. Of the 19 Lancaster bombers that set out, eight failed to return. This pre-strike photograph shows the Moehne Dam with, arrowed, the boom intended to protect the wall against attack by torpedoes.

Opposite page: Post-strike photograph of the Moehne Dam, taken a few hours after the attack by RAF Lancaster bombers using the specially developed bouncing bombs. Water was still pouring through the 240-ft wide breach in the dam wall. The remains of the torpedo boom had been carried through the breach and had come to rest to the right of the patch of turbulent water (arrowed).

Above: The village of Dellwig, seventeen miles along the Ruhr valley from the Moehne Dam, was partially flooded. The embankment for the road crossing the valley was breached in several places (arrowed).

Left: The breached Eder Dam, pictured after the attack by RAF Lancasters.

Above: The Unter Neustadt district of Kassel suffered flooding from the waters released after the Eder Dam was broken.

Right: The Sorpe Dam also suffered damage during the RAF attack, but its packed earth construction withstood the explosions of the bouncing bombs. The post-strike photograph shows damage to the parapet and marks on the rear face of the dam wall caused by the seepage of water.

Above: Junkers 52 transport planes were being assembled at Villacoublay airfield near Paris, scene of a concentrated attack by 101 B-17s of the US 8th Air Force on 14 July 1943. Three bombers failed to return from the attack.

Opposite page: The post-strike photograph of Villacoublay revealed more than 400 bomb craters pockmarking the landing ground and hangars.

The low-altitude attack by 127 B-24 Liberators of the US 8th Air Force, on the complex of oil refineries around Ploesti in Romania on 1 August 1943. It was another epic and costly air operation, with 42 bombers shot down and eight more landing in Turkey with battle damage.

Opposite page, top: B-24s photographed practising low altitude flying over one of their base airfields in Libya, before the attack.

Above: Photo taken during the attack on the Creditul Minier refinery.

Opposite page, bottom: Post-strike photo of the Creditul Minier refinery, showing 12 oil storage tanks and other parts of the plant destroyed

Right: Attack on the Steua-Romana refinery.

Above: The attack on the Astra-Romana refinery.   **Right:** Post-strike photo of the Astra-Romana refinery, showing extensive damage to the plant.

The attack on the Colombia-Aquila refinery, looking west. As fires burn from the bombs dropped by the initial wave, more B-24s run in to deliver their bombs. The cooling tower in the bottom right corner of the photograph, marked 'A', was similarly annotated on the vertical post-strike photograph that follows.

Post-strike photo of the Colombia-Aquila refinery, showing severe damage at several points. The annotations were as follows: 1, cracking and distillation plants destroyed by direct hits; 2, boiler house; 3, direct hits on workshops and compressors; 4, nine oil storage tanks destroyed; 5, large building destroyed; 6, water pumping plant damaged. The cooling tower marked 'A' in the previous photograph can be seen near the top left corner of the photograph.

Left and below left: The Fw 190 assembly plant at Marienburg pictured before and during the concentrated attack by 96 B-17s of the US 8th Air Force on 9 October 1943. The annotations on the photograph were as follows: A, assembly shops; B, hangars; C, flight hangar; D, boiler house; E, store. Pre-strike reconnaissance photographs had revealed only weak anti-aircraft gun defences in position around the target. As a result, bomber crews were ordered to attack at altitudes between 11,000 and 13,000 feet – much lower than usual – to achieve greater bombing accuracy. Due to debris thrown into the air by the bomb detonations and smoke from the fires, photographs taken during the attack gave no clear indication of the amount of damage caused. Two bombers were lost during this attack.

Right: The Marienburg aircraft assembly plant photographed on the day after the attack, showing that many of the buildings had suffered severe damage. What the photograph did not show, however, was that the heavy machine tools and production jigs inside the buildings had survived unless they had taken direct hits. After a rapid clean-up operation, limited production resumed within a few days. By January 1944, production at the plant had been restored to the level before the attack.

Sequence of the attack on the aircraft assembly plant at Brunswick/Waggum by 52 B-17s of the US 8th Air Force, on 11 January 1944. The plant was producing Messerschmitt 110s for the bomber destroyer, night fighter and reconnaissance roles. The bomb bursts shown in photos 1 to 4 all took place within the space of a minute. Twenty minutes after the first wave of bombers attacked, the second wave ran in to bomb; the photo on the right showed the state of the plant before the bombs from the second wave reached the target. Eight bombers were lost from the attack force. For about six weeks after the attack the plant produced no aircraft, but by the end of May 1944 production had returned to pre-attack levels.

A heavy gun battery with four guns, in position southwest of Bremen. The annotations were: A, heavy guns, probably 105 mm; B, light Flak weapons, probably 20 mm; C, Searchlights; D, gunfire predictor; E, Wuerzburg radar for fire control; F, accommodation; G, ammunition storage; H, gun emplacements abandoned, probably used earlier for smaller weapons.

Above: A pair of Flak towers in the Friedrichshain district of Berlin (arrowed). These huge concrete structures, about 90 feet high, were built to provide clear fields of fire for AA guns in built-up areas. The larger tower, on the right, carries four heavy guns, 105 mm or 128 mm, and a similar number of light 20 mm or 37 mm weapons. The smaller tower, on the left, carried the fire control radar, the predictor and the command post as well as a few light AA weapons. The lower storeys of these towers providing space for air raid shelters and civil defence headquarters.

Right: This ground photo of the larger of the two Flak towers at Friedrichshain shows the immense size of this structure.

Top left: Close-up oblique photographs of the various German radar types were necessary, to assist with the technical analysis of their capabilities. Taking these photographs was one of the most difficult and dangerous tasks given to reconnaissance pilots. This well-known photograph depicts the *Wuerzburg* radar at St Bruneval on the north coast of France. The radar was captured in a commando raid on 28 February 1942, and parts of it were brought back to Great Britain for examination.

Bottom left: Following the commando raid on St Bruneval, German radar sites along the Channel Coast became conscious of their vulnerability, and a programme was launched to surround them with barbed wire entanglements. That move made the sites highly conspicuous on aerial photographs.

Top right: *Wuerzburg* Giant fighter control radar pictured on the Dutch island of Walcheren. One of the operators stood helplessly beside the radar as the photographing Spitfire swept past, to become a human yardstick when RAF intelligence officers analysed the picture.

Right: *Seetakt* coast watching radars formed an important part of the German defences to counter the Allied invasion of Northern Europe. Many of these sets were placed on concrete towers, to give them a better view out to sea.

Above: The Deutsche oil refinery near Bremen before camouflage, with the oil storage tanks protected by blast walls.

Right: The same plant after camouflage, the storage tanks covered with netting on a supporting framework to reduce their conspicuous outline.

Opposite page, top: The Hamburg Dammtor railway station before camouflage.

Opposite page, bottom: After camouflage, the station had dummy roads, trees and houses painted on a framework to reduce shadows.

Above: Elaborate camouflage painted on hangars at the Luftwaffe research station at Rechlin near Berlin.

Below: Note that when seen from above, however, the camouflage was ineffective. From above the three dimensional gables had no camouflage effect and the light taxiways showed up clearly.

Opposite page: The big oil hydrogenation plant at Poelitz near Stettin produced petrol from coal, and also converted otherwise unusable crude oils and residues into aviation spirit. The large oil tanks at 'A' have been camouflaged using darkened netting. Other tanks at 'B' had netting and disruptive painting. At 'C' there was a large electric power station.

Above: The decoy situated about 6 miles north of the Poelitz plant. Such decoys were ineffective against daylight attack but at night, if they produced realistic fires, they often looked enticingly like the real thing and collected large numbers of bombs.

Above: The oil refinery beside the River Scheldt near Antwerp. Work had already started to cover the tanks, to make them less conspicuous from the air.

Opposite page: Situated one mile upstream of the Scheldt was this decoy site, with dummy oil storage tanks grouped to resemble the real ones.

Opposite page: The airfield at Nordholz near Cuxhaven showing the runways, taxiways and servicing ramps toned down to make them less conspicuous.

Above: About 3½ miles due north of Nordholz airfield lay its attendant decoy, with the runways, servicing ramps and other features in almost identical positions relative to each other and painted to look conspicuous.

The Hibernia synthetic oil plant at Scholven in the Ruhr industrial area pictured early in the war. The works complex comprised a large coal mine, coke ovens and a power station at A, and the synthetic oil plant at B.

The Hibernia plant later in the war, after the erection of nets decorated with dummy roads and houses at 'C'. The fields at 'D' were covered in dummy houses and roads, to make that area look like a housing estate. The road between E and E1 had been covered by a tunnel of netting.

Complementing the camouflage at the Scholven plant was an elaborate decoy lying on open ground some 2½ miles away to the north, showing the main features of the real plant before it was camouflaged.

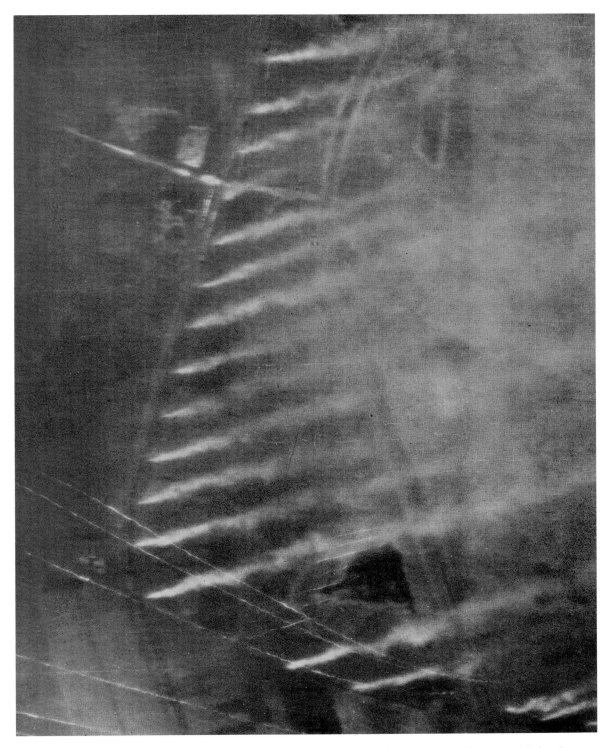

A smoke screen provided an effective defence for the Arado factory aerodrome at Gross Klein near Warnemuende. The smoke generators, positioned about 80 yards apart, were close enough for the smoke trails to fuse together.

Above and right: Heinkel 177 heavy bombers photographed at the Eger aircraft assembly plant, in the Sudentenland territory appropriated from Czechoslovakia by the Germans before the war. This aircraft had been pushed into production prematurely and several failings remained, notably an insufficiently strong wing structure and engines that were liable to overheat and catch fire. After 130 of these bombers had been built, production was halted pending major redesign work on the airframe and engines. Many of the initial production batch ended up dispersed across fields near the assembly plants, without engines. Photographic reconnaissance of these sites revealed the bomber's troubles, and Allied photo interpreters noted: 'Absence of track activity shows that these aircraft have been left in the same position for a considerable time.' Most of the initial production batch remained parked in the fields for the rest of the war, where they helped swell the scores of strafing Allied fighter pilots.

Another aircraft type that ran into production difficulties was the Dornier 217 medium bomber. The Focke Wulf 190 fighter used the a similar BMW 801 engine to that used in early versions of the bomber. By 1943, the need to increase fighter production meant there were insufficient engines for the Do 217s coming off the assembly lines. This photograph shows fields near the Dornier factory at Oberpfaffenhofen in Bavaria, with several Do 217 airframes parked in the open lacking engines. Many of these airframes would remain there for the rest of the war, where they too came under attack from strafing Allied fighters.

The Messerschmitt plant at Regensburg/ Obertraubling, pictured after the US 8th Air Force attack on 25 February 1944. Several large workshops and hangars were heavily damaged.

Following this and other attacks on major aircraft production centres, fighter production was divided into smaller units that could be more easily concealed.

Opposite page: Focke Wulf 189 army co-operation aircraft parked outside the Letov factory near Prague. More than 300 of these aircraft were produced at the plant, before production ended at the beginning of 1943.
Opposite page, inset: Fw 189 in flight.

Above: The airfield at Trondheim/Vaernes in Norway, an important base for four-engined Focke Wulf 200 maritime patrol planes of Kampfgeschwader 40 conducting operations over the north Atlantic.

Right, top and bottom and opposite page: The RAF kept a close eye on the construction progress of the new airfield near Lorient on the French Atlantic coast. The first photo showed the site in August 1940, as preliminary work began. The second photo, taken in June 1941, showed work well advanced on the 2,300-yd runway and the main taxiway cleared. The third photo, taken in early in 1942, showed the work further advanced and a second runway nearing completion. During 1943 the airfield became operational, and served the base for Junkers 88 long-range fighters operating against RAF anti-submarine aircraft over the Bay of Biscay.

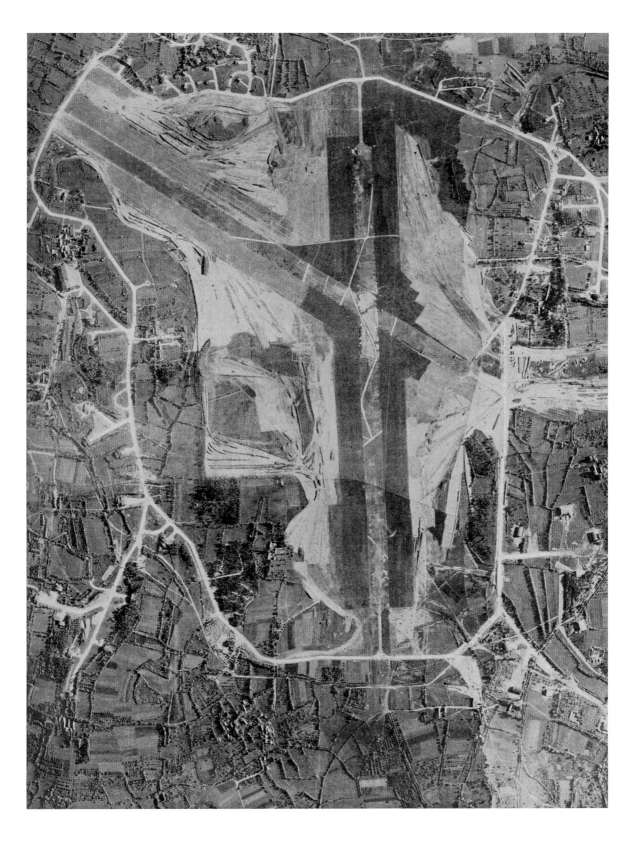

Above: The aircraft dispersal area at the important bomber and night fighter airfield at Venlo in Holland. The planes were dispersed in a wood, with the individual aircraft hangars camouflaged.

Opposite page: Enlargement of the dashed area on the previous photograph, showing a Messerschmitt 110 night fighter parked outside one of the hangars. **Inset:** Ground view of one of the individual aircraft hangars, containing a Ju 88.

Opposite page: Nantes/Chateau Bougon airfield pictured in its original state, when RAF squadrons operated from there in the spring of 1940.

Above: Nantes/Chateau Bougon airfield pictured in 1942, after extensive work to render it suitable for all-weather operations by large aircraft. The original runway had been lengthened, and a second one added. The original hangars had been removed, and several smaller ones were spread over a large area to house individual planes. Elaborate camouflage was then applied to blend the airfield in with the surrounding fields.

Above: T-shaped hangars for individual fighters at Yvrench airfield near Abbeville in France. Although from close-up these structures looked like private houses, when seen from above (inset photograph) it was clear that each one was linked with the main taxiway.

Opposite page: Junkers 88 bombers and reconnaissance aircraft (dark camouflage) and night fighters (light camouflage) seen being prepared for delivery to front-line units, at the aircraft park at Langenau in Bavaria. One night fighter (arrowed) had been jacked into the flying position to have its guns tested on the firing range.

VOLKEL
A/F
IMMED. REPORT K.3111.

Above: This photograph illustrates how difficult it was to render an airfield completely unusable. It shows the Luftwaffe airfield at Volkel in Holland, after the concentrated attack by more than a hundred RAF Lancaster bombers on 3 September 1944. In spite of the airfield's pockmarked appearance, those aircraft dispersed around it which had escaped damage were able to take off to evacuate the base. Bomb craters blocking the main taxiways were filled in, then painted to appear to the casual observer as if they were still there. One aircraft (circled) can be seen getting airborne from a taxiway as this photograph was taken.

Above and right: Caught by accident by the cameras of a high-flying reconnaissance plane above 30,000 feet, these pictures show a low altitude strafing attack by a USAAF Thunderbolt on Brussels/Evere airfield. In the top photograph the low-flying fighter at 'A' (note its proximity to its shadow) was opening fire at a range of about 500 yards on a Messerschmitt 410 at 'C'. At 'B', the bullet strikes on the ground indicated that the initial burst had fallen short. The American pilot corrected his range, and the lower photograph shows the target aircraft on fire.

Left: Giant Me 321 transport gliders pictured at the airfield at Ottingen. The Messerschmitt 110 fighter in the top left corner of the photograph gives scale to the big gliders.

Opposite page, top: Messerschmitt 321 gliders, and the six-engined powered version of this aircraft the Me 323, pictured at Friedrichshafen/ Lowenthal airfield. Also present, arrowed, was a five-engined He 111Z.

Opposite page, bottom: Close-up of the unusual five-engined a Heinkel 111Z, which comprised two He 111 bombers joined by a central wing carrying the fifth engine. This novel aircraft served as a tug for Me 321 transport gliders.

Top and above: Low altitude attack by Beaufighters on the seaplane base at Preveza on the west coast of Greece, in July 1943. The flying boat in the foreground was an Italian Cant Z.501 used for reconnaissance.

Opposite page: Italian-built Savoia Marchetti SM 81 ('A') and SM 82 ('B') three-engined transport aircraft, all wearing German markings, photographed at the airfield at Goslar near Brunswick. Following the Italian surrender in September 1943, these aircraft had been impressed into the Luftwaffe where they equipped four transport Gruppen.

Above: During 1943 the Messerschmitt 410 bomber destroyer, bomber and reconnaissance aircraft went into large-scale production. The smaller photograph showed a few He 177 heavy bombers ('A') and several Me 410s ('B'), at the Luftwaffe airfield at Lechfeld in Bavaria. The larger photograph showed numerous Me 410s outside the Messerschmitt assembly plant at Augsburg. Note the net-covered aircraft shelters, and the dummy trees positioned throughout the area to give it a rustic look.

Opposite page, top: Prague/Ruzyne airfield, photographed in February 1945. At first glance, the aircraft look like standard Junkers 88s. However, the shadows betray them as Mistel combination aircraft each with an Fw 190 fighter mounted on top.

Opposite page bottom: Close up of the Mistel combination aircraft, comprising a Ju 88 fitted with an large explosive warhead in place of the cabin, and an Fw 190 fighter rigidly mounted above it. The Fw 190 pilot aligned the combination on the target, then released the Ju 88 which continued on that path to impact. The Fw 190 then made good its escape.

Above: Dramatic low-altitude reconnaissance photograph taken by Pilot Officer J. Chandler of the PRU, as his Spitfire flew past the heavy cruiser *Admiral Hipper* in dry dock at Brest in January 1941.

Opposite page: German minesweepers seen carrying out a methodical sweep outside a port. Each boat towed two paravanes to cut the tethering cables of moored mines. The wave patterns indicated that the craft were steaming at 11 knots.

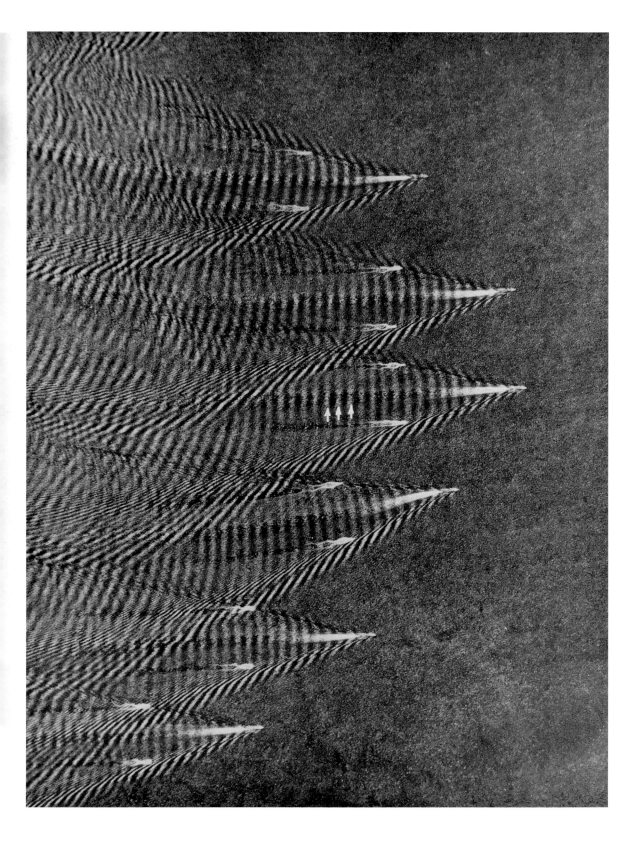

Above: The dry dock in the port of St Nazaire was the only one on the French Atlantic coast large enough to take the German battleship *Tirpitz*. On 28 March 1942 British forces launched a major raid to put the dock out of action. The old destroyer HMS *Campbeltown*, loaded with explosives, was rammed into the lock gate (arrowed). Also commandos landed, and blew up several key installations.

Opposite page: The dry dock at St Nazaire pictured after the raid, with the lock gate 'A', badly buckled and dislodged from its sill, lying along the side of the lock.

Above: The dry dock at St Nazaire pictured ten months after the raid. German engineers had built a dam at the outer end of the entrance lock, and another at the inner wall of the dock. The facility would remain unusable for large ships for the remainder of the war.

Opposite page: In February 1942 the battle cruiser *Gneisenau* suffered severe damage to her bow area during an RAF attack on Kiel harbour, which led to her being decommissioned. She was seen here later in the year (arrowed, centre) in the floating dock at Gdynia, Poland, with the front 140 feet of her bow and her heavy armament removed. At the bottom of the photograph was the aircraft carrier *Graf Zeppelin* (also arrowed), on which construction work had ceased. The RAF kept both warships under regular watch, for signs of a resumption of work to bring them into service.

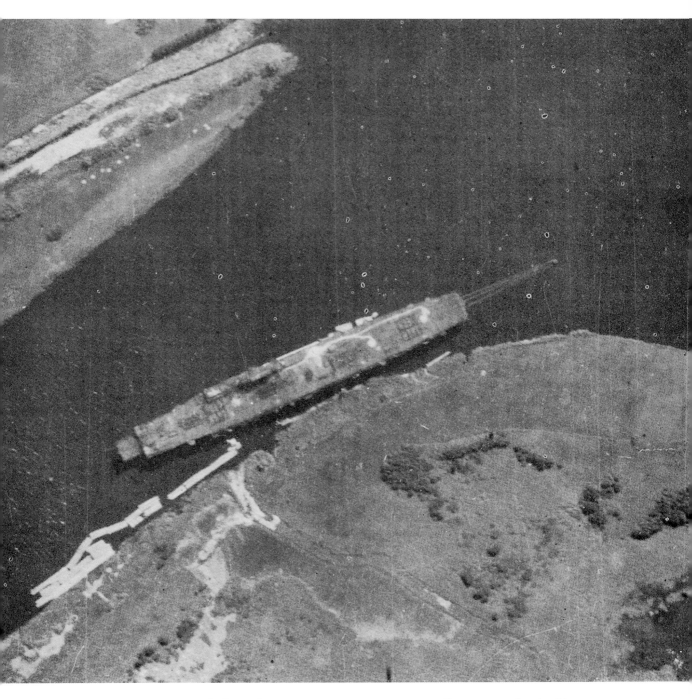

Opposite page: A later photograph showed *Gneisenau* after leaving the floating dock, with her main armament removed and the process of dismantling further advanced.

Above: The aircraft carrier *Graf Zeppelin* photographed abandoned in a backwater near Stettin in May 1943. She sat at anchor beside an undeveloped marshy island, and there were no signs of work in progress. *Graf Zeppelin* remained at Stettin until Soviet forces neared the port in 1945, when she was scuttled. The aircraft carrier was raised in 1947, but capsized and sank while under tow to the Soviet Union.

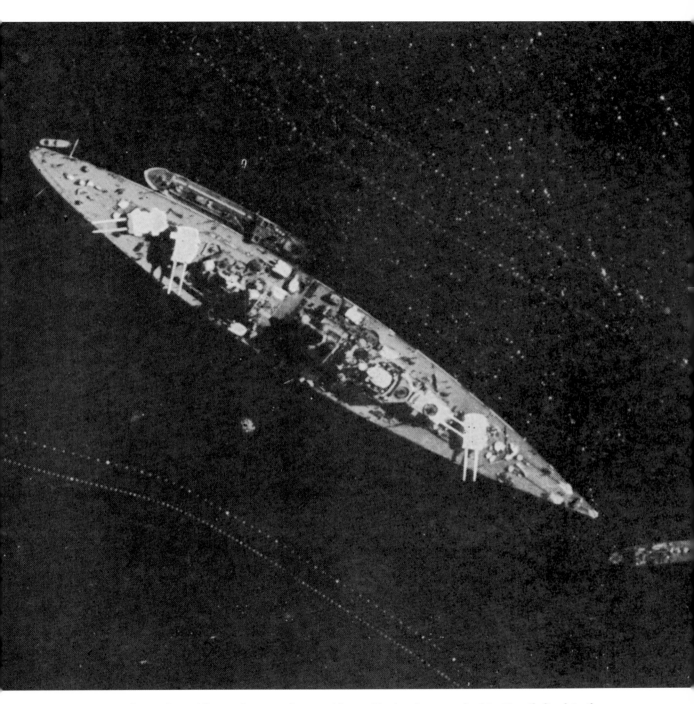

Opposite page: A daring low oblique photograph, taken from about 200 feet, of the battleship *Tirpitz* anchored in Aas Fjord, Norway, in March 1942. Because she represented a major danger to British convoys carrying military supplies to the Soviet Union, the warship's movements were carefully monitored by the Allied intelligence services.

Above: *Tirpitz* photographed in Narvik fjord in the north of Norway, in July 1942, protected by anti-torpedo nets.

Above: As Allied ground forces advanced through France in August 1944, German warship at ports along the Bay of Biscay made desperate efforts to escape. Photo shows the destroyer Z 24 and a torpedo boat under cannon and rocket attack from Beaufighters of Nos 236 and 404 Squadrons, off Bordeaux on 24 August. Both vessels were sunk.

Below: Dramatic photo as Beaufighters of Nos 144, 254, 455 and 489 Squadrons delivering a concentrated attack on German minesweepers operating off the Dutch coast on 25 August 1944. Minesweeper M 347 was sunk and other vessels suffered damage.

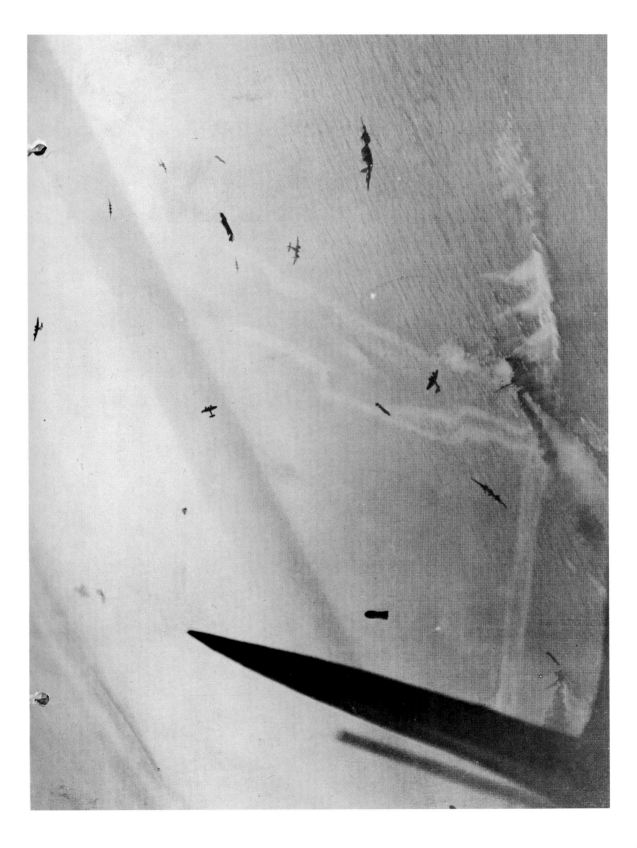

Attack by Beaufighters of Nos 144 and 404 Squadrons on the freighter *Inger Johanne* off Kristiansand, Norway, on 15 October 1944, which left the ship burning. A post-strike photograph taken three days later (below) showed the vessel aground with only a small part of her superstructure above water, but it was still burning.

Opposite page: As the threat of an Allied invasion became clear, the Luftwaffe rendered unusable several airfields close to the coast of northern Europe that were liable to capture. This photograph showed the airfield at Crepon, 12 miles north-west of Caen in Normandy, with a grid-like arrangement of mounds and trenches to prevent take-offs and landings.

Above: Close up of the airfield at Crepon, showing how it had been divided into unusable sections. The decision to render the airfield unusable was vindicated on D-Day, when Crepon and the surrounding area were overrun by British troops on the morning of the invasion.

Opposite page: Long-range guns at Cap Gris Nez, mounted for coastal defence but also used to fire across the English Channel at targets in Kent. Had the Allies decided to land at that part of the coast, this battery would have been an important obstacle to overcome. The three super-heavy 30.5 cm (12-in) guns were mounted in concrete emplacements at 'A'. At 'B' were three dummy gun positions following a similar layout. On the cliff edge, at 'C', were three smaller guns in open emplacements, and a further position for six guns at 'D'.

Above: Close-up of the three-gun coastal defence position at Cap Gris Nez, in front of the lighthouse.

Below: Beach obstacles, some of them holding explosive charges, set up on the beach below the high-tide mark between Ostend and Dunkirk.

Opposite page: 'Hedgehog' anti-invasion obstacles laid out on the sand, with rows of stakes to seaward. In the middle of the photograph was a horse used to transport the obstacles, its rider lying flat beside it fearing attack.

Opposite page: The Luftwaffe airfield at Gael near Rennes, under attack from Mosquito fighter-bombers of the 2nd Tactical Air Force. The photographing aircraft was part of the Flak-suppression force, and one of its bombs can be seen bursting beside a Flak position.

Above and below: Other photographs taken during the attack on Gael airfield, with bomb explosions developing from hits on the large hangars.

Above: Once the invasion began, the German army would need to depend on the French railway system to move many of its combat units and supplies to the battle zone. Beforehand, therefore, the Allied air attacks were concentrated on railway repair shops and marshalling yards to disrupt the system. Photograph showed the important marshalling yard at Trappes south west of Paris, after the attack by 261 Halifax and Mosquito bombers of RAF Bomber Command on the night of 6/7 March 1944. No aircraft were lost. The arrows show the destruction and derailment of items of rolling stock and severe damage to the engine shed.

Opposite page: The marshalling yard at Amiens/Longueau, pictured after the attack by 140 RAF bombers on 15/16 March 1944 and by 130 bombers on the following night. Three bombers were lost during the two raids.

ISY M/Y. BEFORE

Opposite page: The marshalling yard at Juvisy near Paris, pictured before and after the attack by 209 RAF bombers on the night of 18/19 April 1944 which inflicted severe damage. One bomber was lost.

Above: The large barracks and military training ground at Mailly-le-Camp near Paris, severely damaged after the attack by 362 RAF bombers on the night of 3/4 May 1944. On this occasion, German night fighters arrived in the area after the target had been marked but before the main attack began. As a result, what should have been an easy 'milk run' attack for the bomber crews ended with one of the RAF's heaviest proportionate loss rates of the war: 42 bombers were lost.

THE BATTLE OF NORMANDY

Opposite page: The first reliable information to reach Allied senior commanders in England, on the progress of the Normandy landings, came from photographic reconnaissance aircraft. Taken on the morning of D-Day, this vertical photograph showed landing craft unloading British troops on Sword Beach to the west of Ouistreham. Note the long column of vehicles heading for the beach exit points at the bottom of the photograph.

Below: High-altitude oblique photograph showing activity by ships and landing craft off Gold Beach near Asnelles.

Opposite page: Oblique photograph taken on the morning of D-day, showing Horsa troop-carrying gliders and a single larger Hamilcar (arrowed, bottom right), lying on open land immediately to the east of the Caen Canal. Many of the gliders had their noses or tails detached, to facilitate the unloading of vehicles or heavy weapons.

Right: Three LSTs (Landing Ships, Tank) unloading vehicles and supplies for British troops on Gold Beach at Graye-sur-Mer on D-Day+1, 7 June.

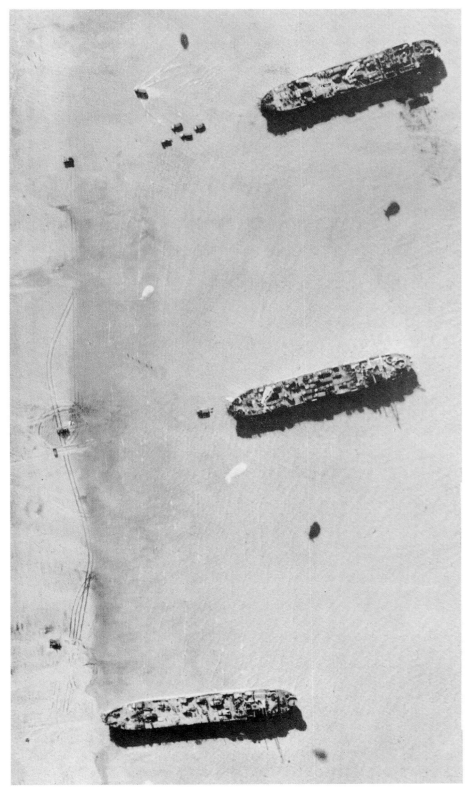

Opposite page: During the weeks before the invasion, and after it, Allied bombers mounted a campaign against bridges over the River Seine with the aim of isolating the landing area in Normandy from the rest of France. Photograph shows the Port du Graviere rail bridge to the south of Rouen, with one span dropped.

Above: The rail bridge at Rouen/Oissel, with one span dropped. In a later attack the parallel road bridge, nearer the camera, was also wrecked.

Below: Rouen/Sotteville rail bridge with one span dislodged and in the river.

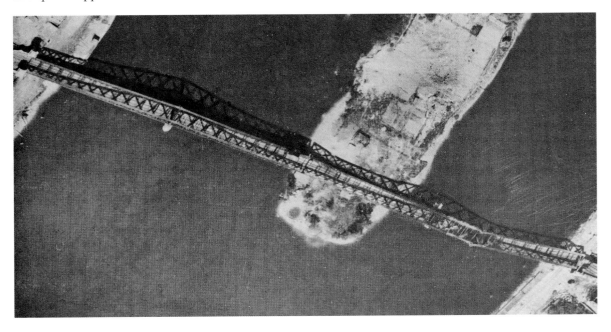

Above: Aerial view of a land action in progress. Taken near Caen, this photograph shows British tanks and motor vehicles advancing over open country. To cross the road the vehicles converged to cross at points that had been cleared of mines. Note the large number of blast marks from exploding shells and mines.

Opposite page: British tanks in action near Caen. The vehicles left characteristic track marks when they turned or reversed to manoeuvre into position.

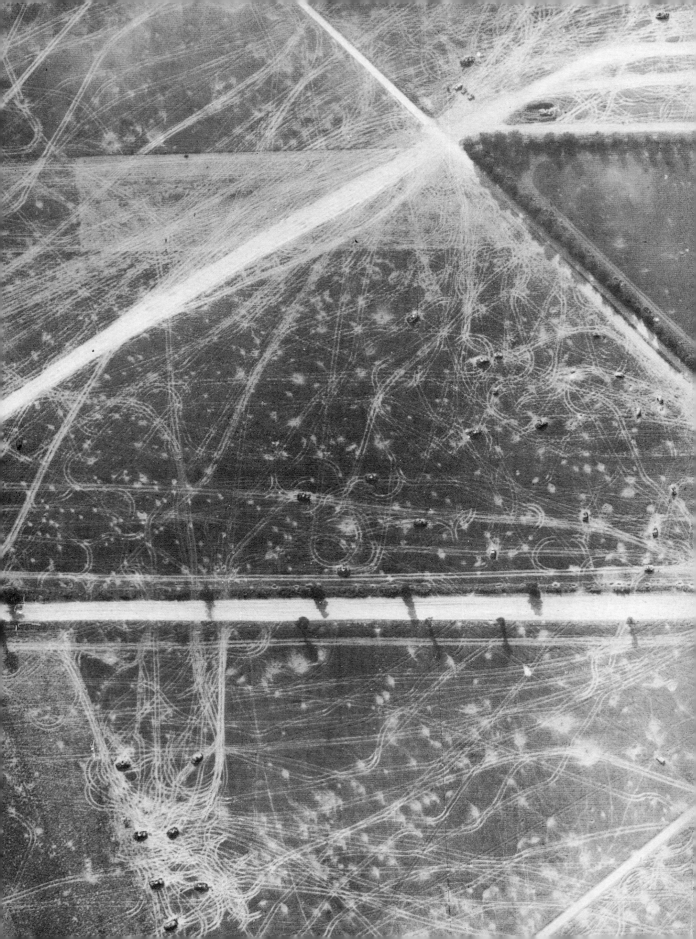

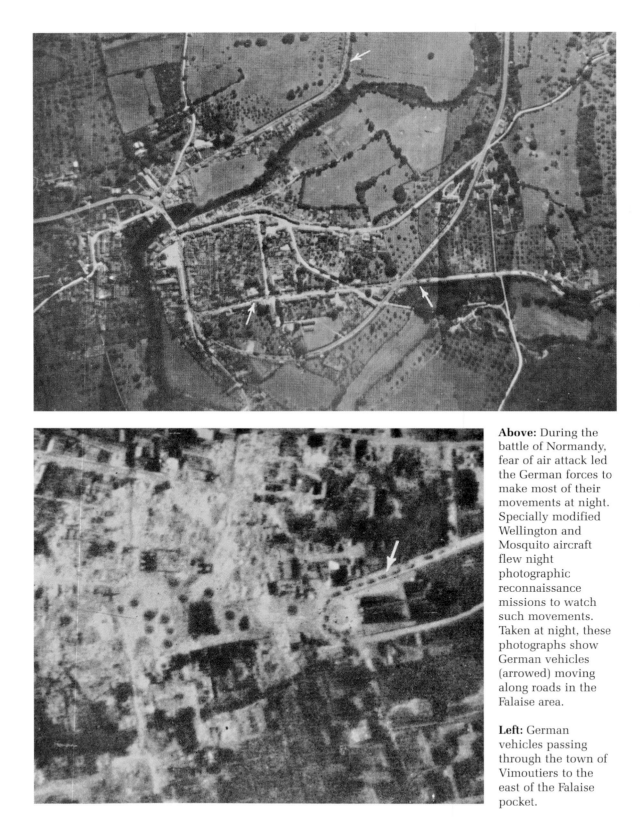

Above: During the battle of Normandy, fear of air attack led the German forces to make most of their movements at night. Specially modified Wellington and Mosquito aircraft flew night photographic reconnaissance missions to watch such movements. Taken at night, these photographs show German vehicles (arrowed) moving along roads in the Falaise area.

Left: German vehicles passing through the town of Vimoutiers to the east of the Falaise pocket.

Above: Bridge at Chateaubourg on the main road running from Marseilles through the Rhone Valley ('A'), destroyed by French partisans. The line of German military vehicles escaping to the north, arrowed, was forced to travel at low speed along the main rail line running through the area.

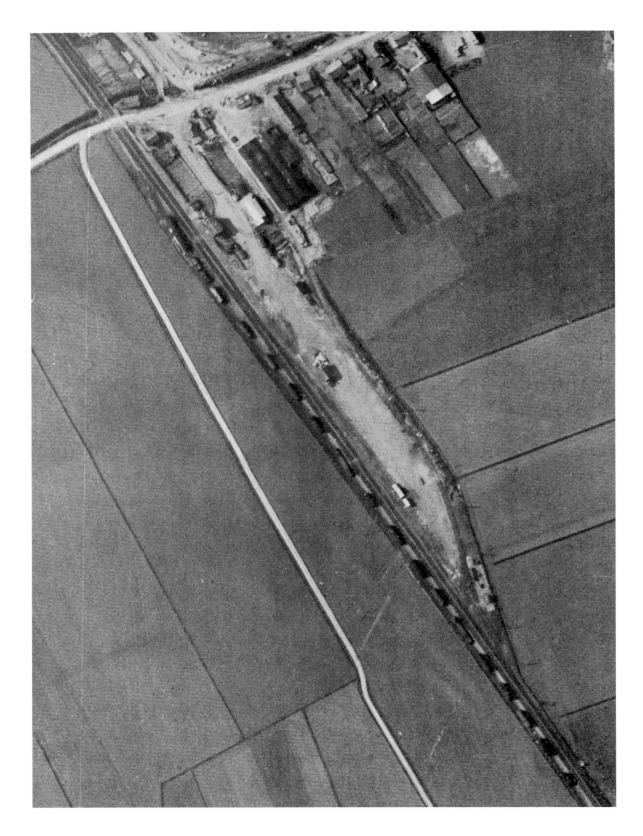

Opposite page: German military train stopped on the line between Calais and Dunkirk, with the trucks uncoupled and spaced out. Probably the trucks carried ammunition, and were spaced out so that if one exploded for any reason it would not set off others.

Above: With many bridges in France rendered unusable by the Allied air attacks, the German army resorted to 'underwater bridges' to move troops and vehicles across some smaller rivers. These might consist of large-diameter concrete drainage pipes lowered into the river parallel to the direction of flow, to produce a shallow water path a few inches deep. Alternatively pontoons might be sunk to rest on the bottom of a shallow river, with the same intention. To avoid detection, these crossings were used only at night or in poor visibility. This underwater bridge ('A') was spotted by a keen-eyed photographic interpreter in the River Somme 4 miles south of Abbeville. The 'give away' was the well-used track seemingly leading to nothing on the riverbank. Note the conspicuous dummy crossings at 'B' and 'C'.

LAUNCHING PLATFORM

Above and left: The original fixed-type V.1 launching sites were constructed to a common pattern, like this example situated at Bois Carre near Abbeville in northern France (inset photograph shows the site under construction). Once Allied photo interpreters know what to look for, these sites were easy to find and during the early months of 1944 they came under heavy attack from the air. The larger photograph shows the Bois Carre site after it had been attacked and abandoned. The three distinctive 'ski' shaped buildings (arrowed at 'A') were used to store flying bombs after delivery to the site. The launching platform, also arrowed, was aligned on London.

Opposite page: Another fixed V.1 launching site, pictured after it had been attacked and abandoned.

Above and below: To make location more difficult, Luftwaffe engineers developed a new and simpler type of V.1 launching site without the distinctive 'ski' shaped buildings. The new launching sites used prefabricated components, which the site crew could assemble quickly and replace easily if items were damaged. The new type of launching ramp (at 'A') was simpler in design and easier to camouflage than its predecessor. The specialised buildings necessary to prepare the missiles for firing were hidden in woods or orchards, and wherever possible existing barns were used to house missiles and equipment. In the lower picture, the camouflaged launching ramp was just visible at 'B'.

Top right: Flying bomb positioned on its ramp, ready for launching.

FLYING BOMB ON LAUNCHING PLATFORM

Right: A flying bomb in flight on its way to England.

Below: Gun camera photos of a flying bomb under attack from an RAF fighter.

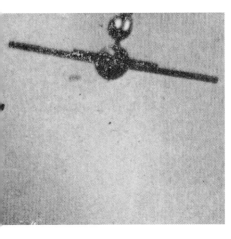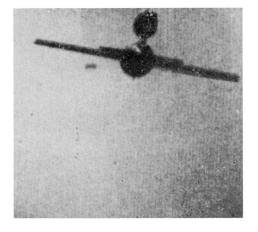

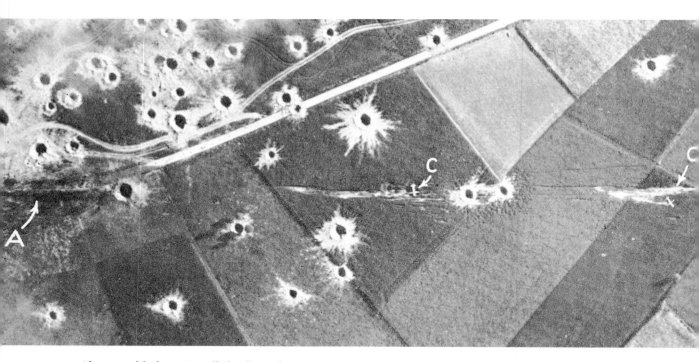

Above and below: Not all the flying bombs launched got airborne. In these photographs, 'A' points to the launching ramp. 'B' shows the scars where the V.1s had skidded across the ground, then the shallow crater and blast mark where a warhead had detonated. Note the difference in appearance between the deeper craters caused by bomb from attacking Allied planes, and the more shallow craters with blast marks from the V.1 explosions. 'C' points to V.1s that had failed to attain flying speed, but which also failed to detonate after skidding across the ground.

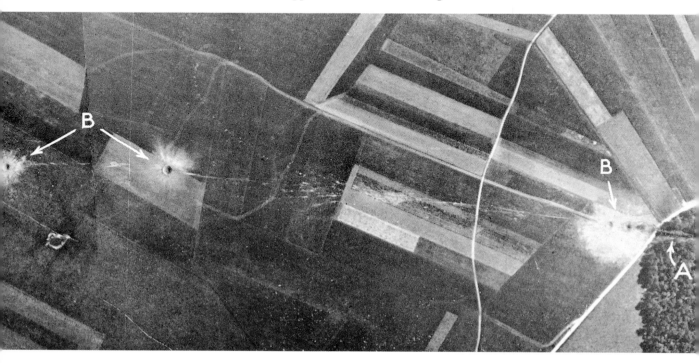

Right: Usually shadows were a hindrance to photo interpreters, but on occasions they could be a help. The clever use of camouflage netting on a German destroyer tied up at Bordeaux concealed its outline when seen from above. The shadows cast by the low spring sun revealed the subterfuge, however.

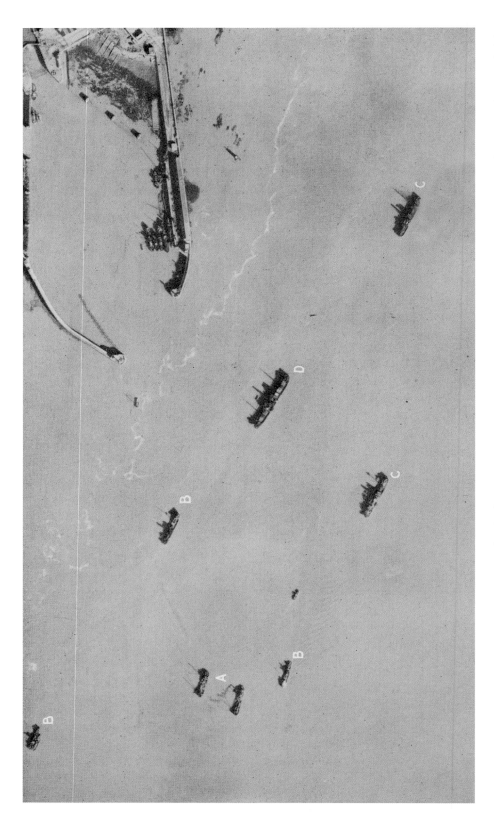

Left: Had this vertical photograph been taken in normal lighting conditions, it would have been more difficult to identify the different types of vessel in this German convoy. The shadows reveal the identity of the leading vessels, the two small coasters at 'A' with aft-mounted engines and funnels, and the three armed trawlers at 'B' with long foredecks. Sailing with them at 'C' were two armed merchant ships and a large merchant ship ('D').

Opposite page: In this vertical photograph of the city of Cologne, the shadows reveal the structural features of the two large bridges carrying traffic over the River Rhine.

Left: Railway viaducts made lucrative targets for air attack, since damage to the structure would often halt traffic for several months until repairs had been completed. This photograph showed the viaduct over the River Aulne at Chatealin in Brittany, France. Although the supports of the 390-yd long structure were not visible from directly above, the shadows revealed these clearly.

Opposite page: The viaduct carrying the Paris to Le Havre main line over the valley at Mirville, about 16 miles west of the Le Havre. Again, the shadows show clearly the supports for the structure.

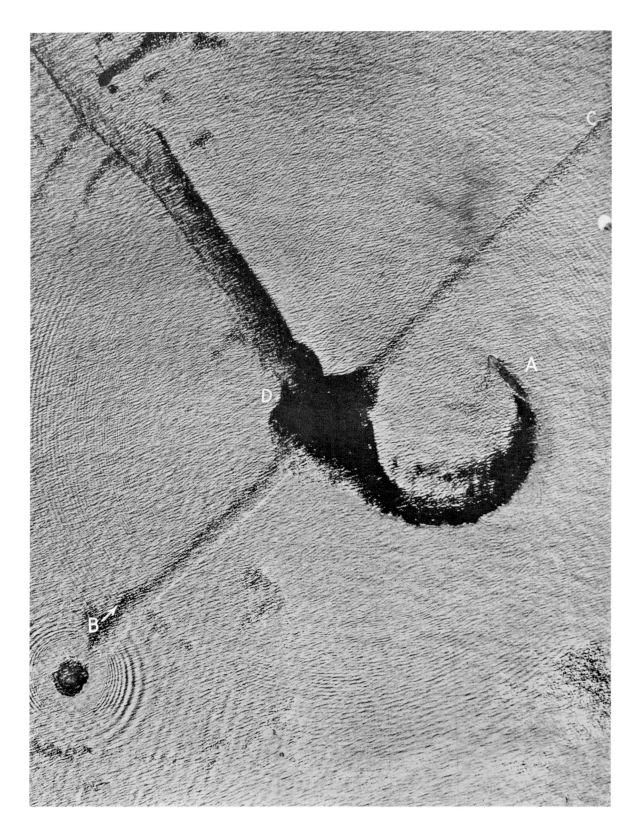

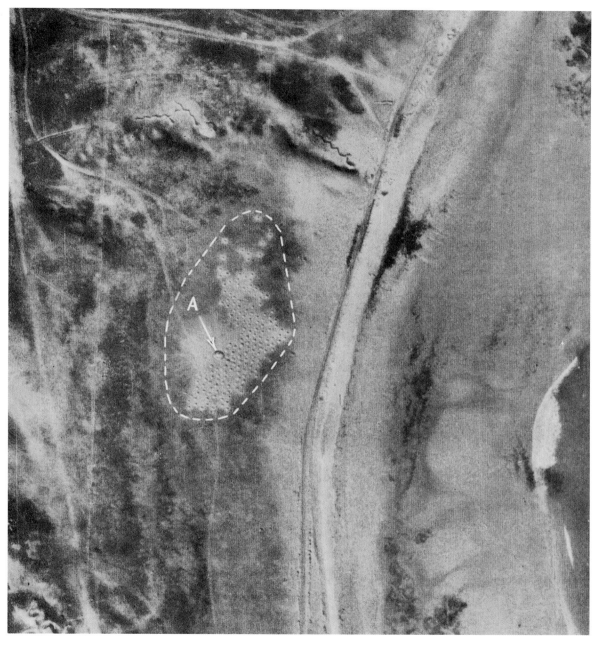

Opposite page: Dramatic photograph taken in June 1943 from a high flying reconnaissance Spitfire over the Straits of Messina between Italy and Sicily, after its pilot had noticed unusual activity below. The line from the top left-hand corner to the centre of the page was the wake left by an Italian motor vessel. A British submarine at 'B' had launched a salvo of torpedoes, and at point 'D' one torpedo hit the motor vessel and exploded. Seriously damaged, the vessel turned to port and quickly lost speed, coming almost to a halt at 'A'. The remaining torpedoes continued on their course to point 'C'. Shortly after this photograph was taken, the motor vessel blew up and sank.

Above: Part of the coastline near the port of Lorient in France. During an attack on the port a stray bomb landed at 'A' in a minefield, and exploded to set off about 150 mines by sympathetic detonation.

Right: Surrealistic patterns in the sky, captured by a long-exposure photograph taken during the Bomber Command attack on Hamburg on the night of 29/30 July 1943. The lines were caused by the passage of tracer rounds from automatic Flak weapons. The rotation of the individual rounds caused the 'waviness' of the lines.

Bottom right: A picture that puzzled photo interpreters for a time. This winter shot of Oslo Fjord revealed a channel clear of ice, linking the city of Oslo with the nearby Langoen Island. To keep that channel clear of ice meant there had to be almost continual traffic passing through it. That meant the island contained something of importance, though from aerial photographs it was impossible to determine what. Conversations with expatriate Norwegians with knowledge of the city quickly resolved the mystery, however. Lagoen Island was the city of Oslo's refuse dump! The moral was clear: when examining aerial photographs, interpreters had always to consider the possibility that the 'unidentified object' under examination might be associated with some quite mundane aspect of human activity.

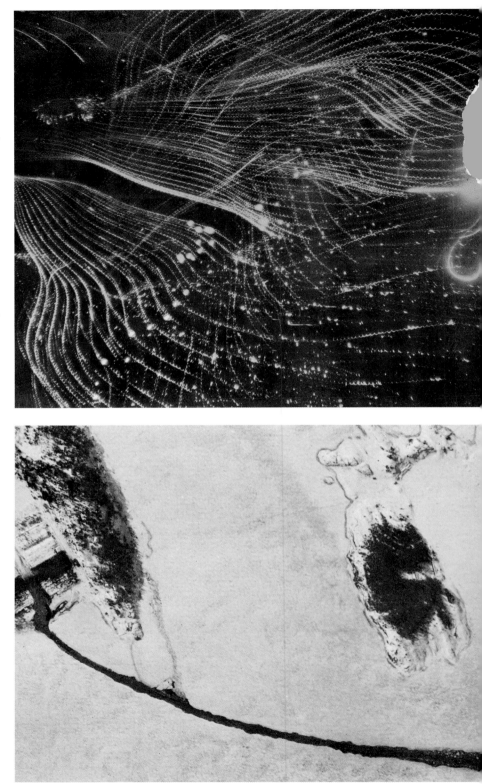